I0467371

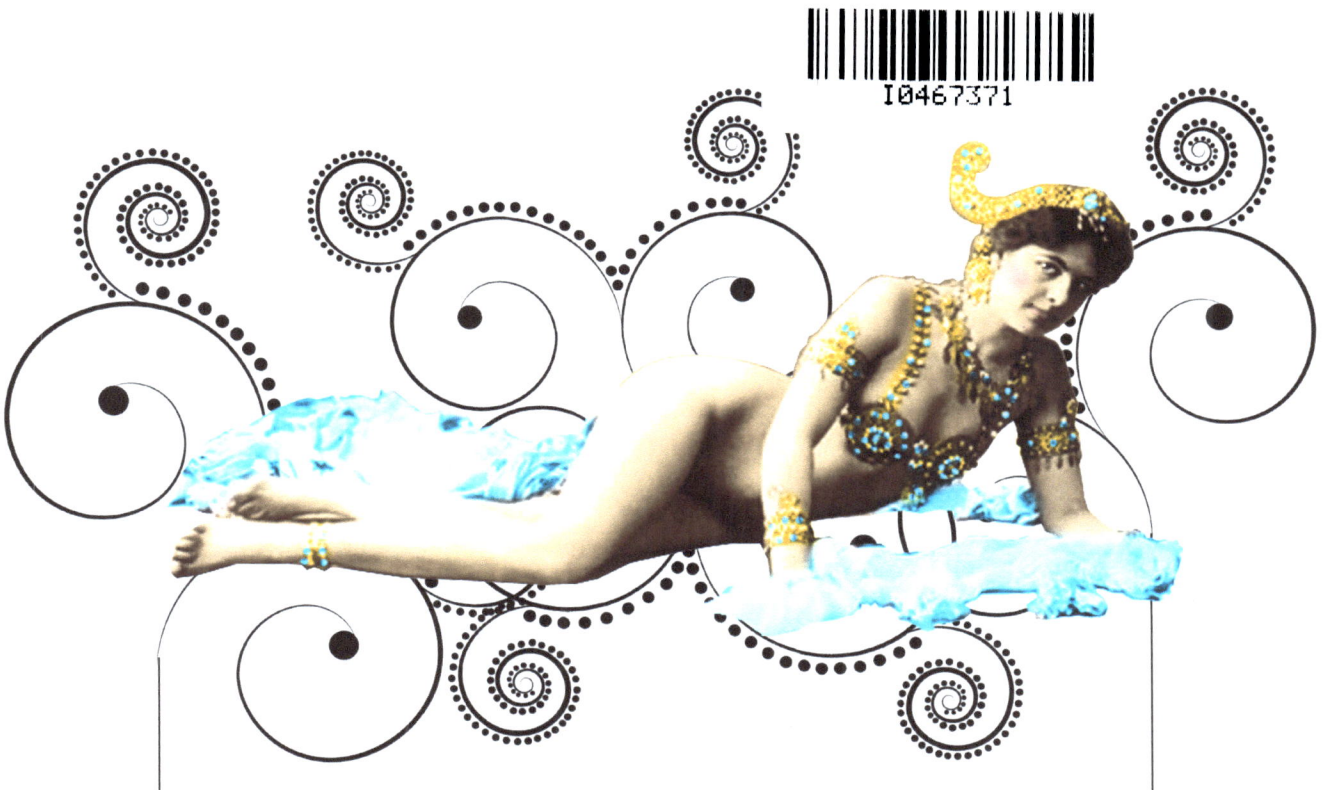

This issue of Bad Influence was funded on Kickstarter. It could not have been created without the help of these brave backers:

Lynda Underwood
Maxine Bevin
Barbe Saint John
Nicole Franczvai
Dwight Bishop
Eduardo Mercado
Leodis Sharpe
Jennifer Cahoon
Denise Hunter
Terry Dee Yackley
Patricia waldorf
Black Denim Lit
Esta Beerman-Price
Louise Foster
Joanne Dennis
Carolyn Brady
Mary Pendergrass
Adriann Sims-Harris
Patricia Hendricks
Laura Rajsic-Lanier
Meta Anna Campbell

Maude Leake
Alice Segura
Hope Leman
Elly Vitullo
Julie Ousley
Dayle Persons
Angela Zacharek
Kelly Harms
Cindy Couling
Carolyn Huber
Anne Grappo
LA Smith
Marilyn Noah
Luna Doyle Oberg
Cindy Blood
Kara Hayes Bosch
Corinne Stubson
Lisa G Miller
Heidi Orndorff
Sally Hackney
Jill Minehart

Thanks so much for making it happen!

Artists in This Issue

Cindy Couling
Sunnyvale, California

Cindy Couling is a professional artist, illustrator and designer. She expresses her whimsical, colorful style in a variety of media including pencil crayon, ceramics, watercolor, pen and ink and whatever medium strikes her fancy. Cindy enjoys observing people and incorporating their unique expressions and personalities into her work. You can see more of her work at Couling.com.

Jean Mirre
Nantiat, France

Jean Mirre paints with oil, acrylic, and ink on large canvases. He has been making physical collages for many years, and has extended his skill to digital work. Jean uses images as words to write wordless modern poetry. You can see more of his artwork on his Facebook page.

Jackie Beeman
Redlands, California

Jackie Beeman started scrapbooking in 1990, when her first grandchild was born. A decade later, she discovered art journaling. She likes to do sketches and paint faces. More of her work can be found on her blog at beemanpencilnpaints.wordpress.com.

Jennifer Gillooly Cahoon
East Providence, Rhode Island

Jennifer Gillooly Cahoon is a teacher and painter living and working in New England. She is currently immersed in a series of work depicting well-known figures in such a way that speaks to the core of their being. She utilizes the symbolism of the Dia de Los Muertos tradition as a vehicle to reveal the inner essence of her subjects. More of her work can be seen on her web site, JGCahoon.com.

Barbe Saint John
Cleveland, Ohio

Barbe Saint John is a mixed media artist, jewelry maker, metalsmith, author, instructor and self-proclaimed creativity junkie. More of her work can be seen on her Facebook page, Modernist Metal.

Lisa Vollrath
Euless, Texas

Lisa Vollrath is a prolific mixed-media artist, writer and designer. She teaches classes and designs products for Ten Two Studios, the company she started in 2005. Her current work can always been seen on her ever-growing web site, LisaVollrath.com.

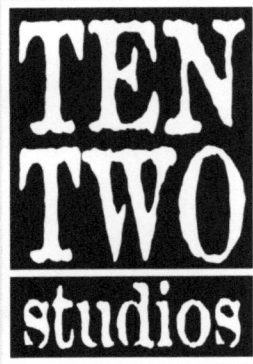

**Visit online at
TenTwoStudios.com
or email at
TenTwoStudios
@yahoo.com**

A Few Words From Lisa

When I decided to put this issue of Bad Influence together, I wasn't really sure where I was headed. I didn't have a theme, so I took a poll of my readers, and Notorious Woman won.

For many years, my own artwork has been focused on women. It's not some big political or social statement. I just find women more interesting to illustrate. Even when I'm grabbing collage images, I gravitate towards female rather than male.

When I put together the call for art, I thought I knew what this issue was going to be. I made a list of possible subjects for artists to consider, and very quickly, I started receiving questions about other women that might be included. The list of notorious women grew quite lengthy.

As the artwork started to arrive in my inbox, I set out to learn a little something about each woman the participating artists chose as their subjects. I made notes, and included them in this issue, along with quotes from or about each woman. I learned a lot, and I hope you will, too.

This is the ninth issue of Bad Influence, and probably the only one for 2014. I hope you enjoy it as much as I enjoyed putting it together...

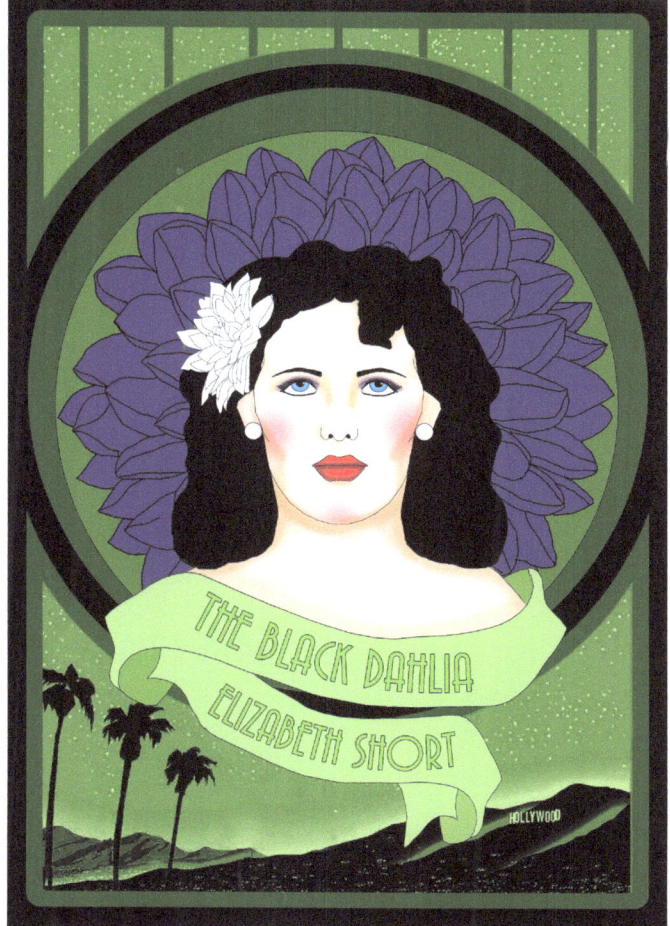

Elizabeth Short
Lisa Vollrath

Digital illustration for
4" X 6" postcards.

Controversy is part of the nature of art and creativity.

Yoko Ono

Yoko Ono is a Japanese artist, singer, songwriter, and activist. She has been criticized for her influence over late husband John Lennon and his music, and blamed for the breakup of the Beatles. Although her name is often used to indicate an evil female influence, she has worked tirelessly since her husband's death to keep his memory, and his quest for a peaceful world, alive. She promotes her creative work and shares inspirational messages and images on Twitter, Instagram, and Facebook.

The Difficulty of Dreaming Alone
Cindy Couling

Watercolor, ink and inkjet printing on paper.
8" x 10"

From the artist: *Even though John Lennon was taken from Yoko far too early, he is still the air she breathes and the dream she dreams every night. She keeps him alive.*

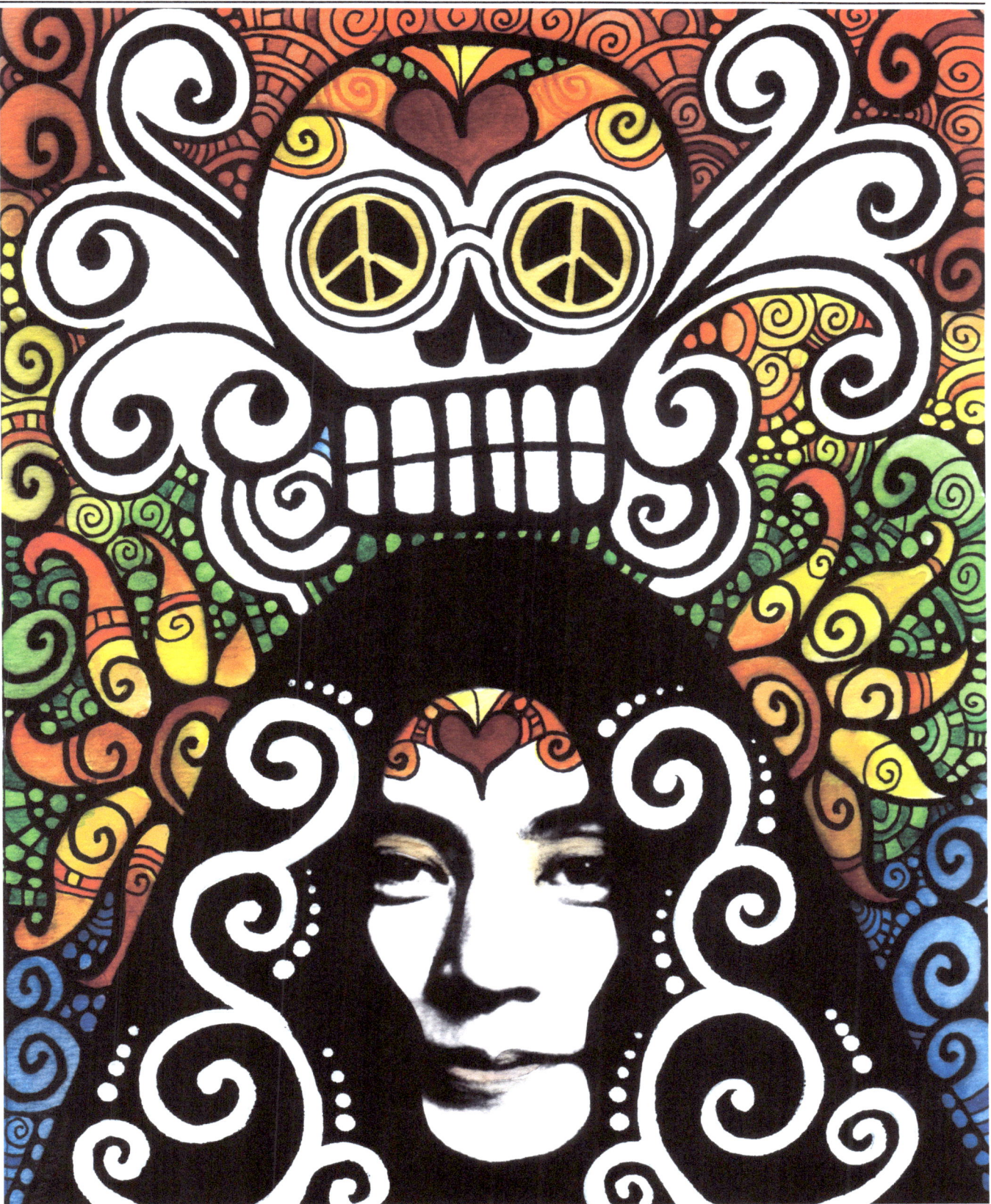

What this country needs is more unemployed politicians.

Angela Davis

Angela Davis is an American political activist, scholar and author. During the 1960s, she was a prominent counterculture activist, a leader of the Communist Party in the US, and was associated with the Black Panther party. She spent several months in 1970 on the FBI Most Wanted Fugitive list, and President Richard Nixon called her a dangerous terrorist when she was finally arrested. She is now a retired professor from the History of Consciousness Department at the University of California, Santa Cruz, and a former director of the university's Feminist Studies department.

Revolution is a Serious Thing
Cindy Couling

Watercolor, ink and inkjet printing on paper.
8" x 10"

From the artist: *Angela Davis is an iconic face of black politics in America in the early 70's. Davis once said: "It is both humiliating and humbling to discover that a single generation after the events that constructed me as a public personality, I am remembered as a hairdo."*

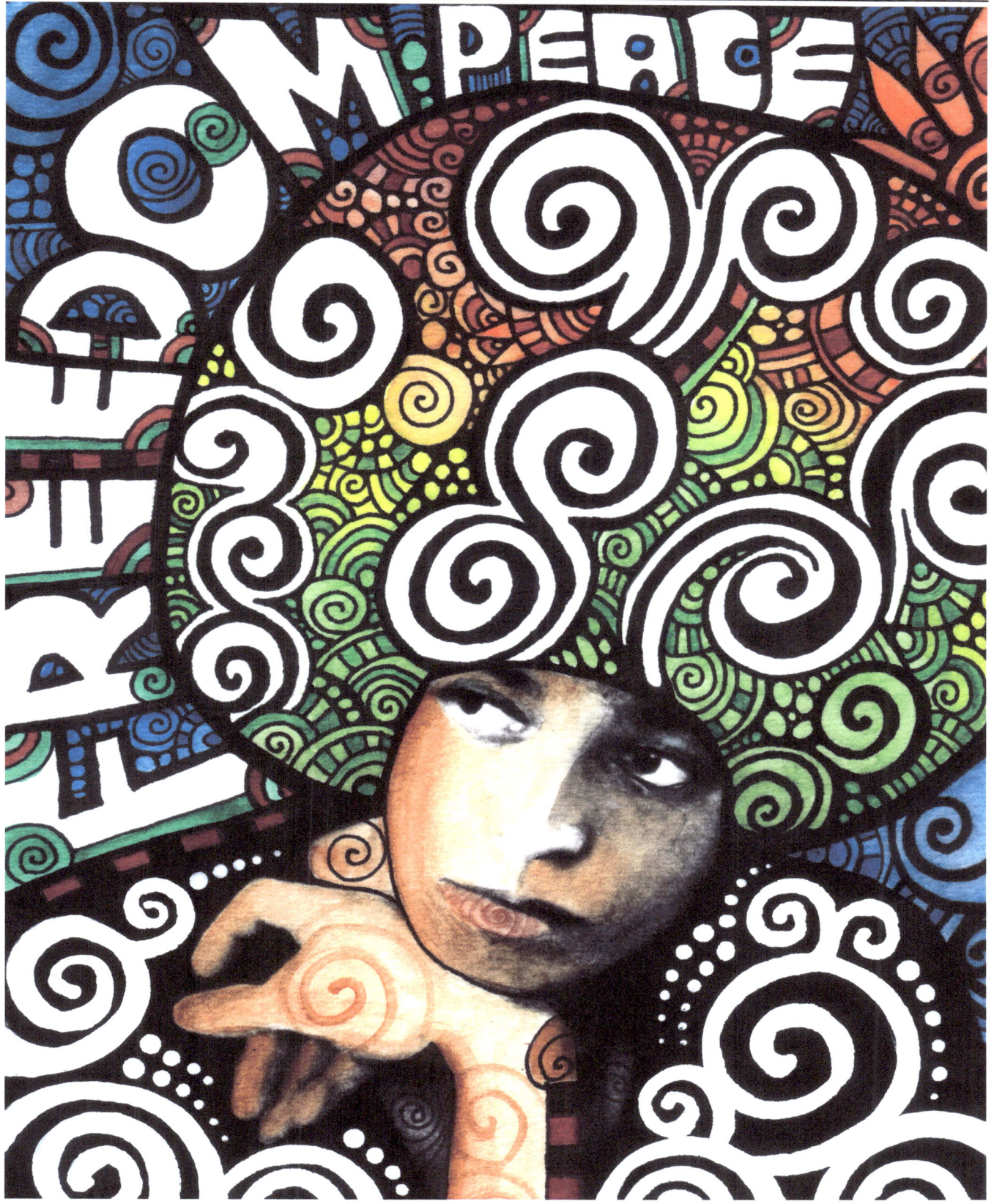

It's very expensive to be me.
It's terrible the things I have to do to be me.

Anna Nicole Smith

Anna Nicole Smith was an American model, actress and television personality. She first gained popularity by posing for Playboy, and was named Playmate of the year in 1993. She became the face of Guess jeans, and modeled for Lane Bryant. In 1994, 26 year-old Smith married 89 year-old oil tycoon J. Howard Marshall. 14 months later, Marshall died, and within weeks, his family began a legal battle over the estate that would last for the rest of Smith's life and beyond. In 2006, she had daughter Dannielynn, and a few days later, her son Daniel, from her first marriage, died in her hospital room. Six months later, after relentless focus on her son's death by the press, she died of a drug overdose. The legal battle over her estate, and the paternity of her daughter, also played out in the tabloids for months after her death.

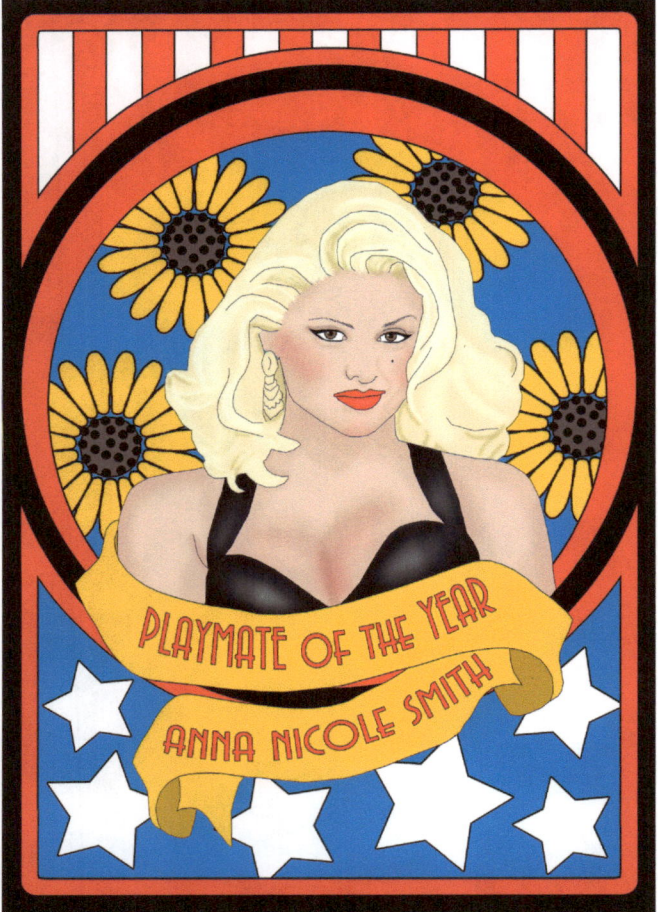

Anna Nicole
Lisa Vollrath

Digital illustration for
4" X 6" postcards.

Anna Nicole Smith, Dia de Los Muertos
Jennifer Gillooly Cahoon

Water miscible oil paint on linen.
16"x 20"

From the artist: *Anna Nicole Smith gained early fame as a model for Guess and Playboy magazine. Here, she is depicted as the wild, glamorous party girl she was-- decked out in red and ready to party.*

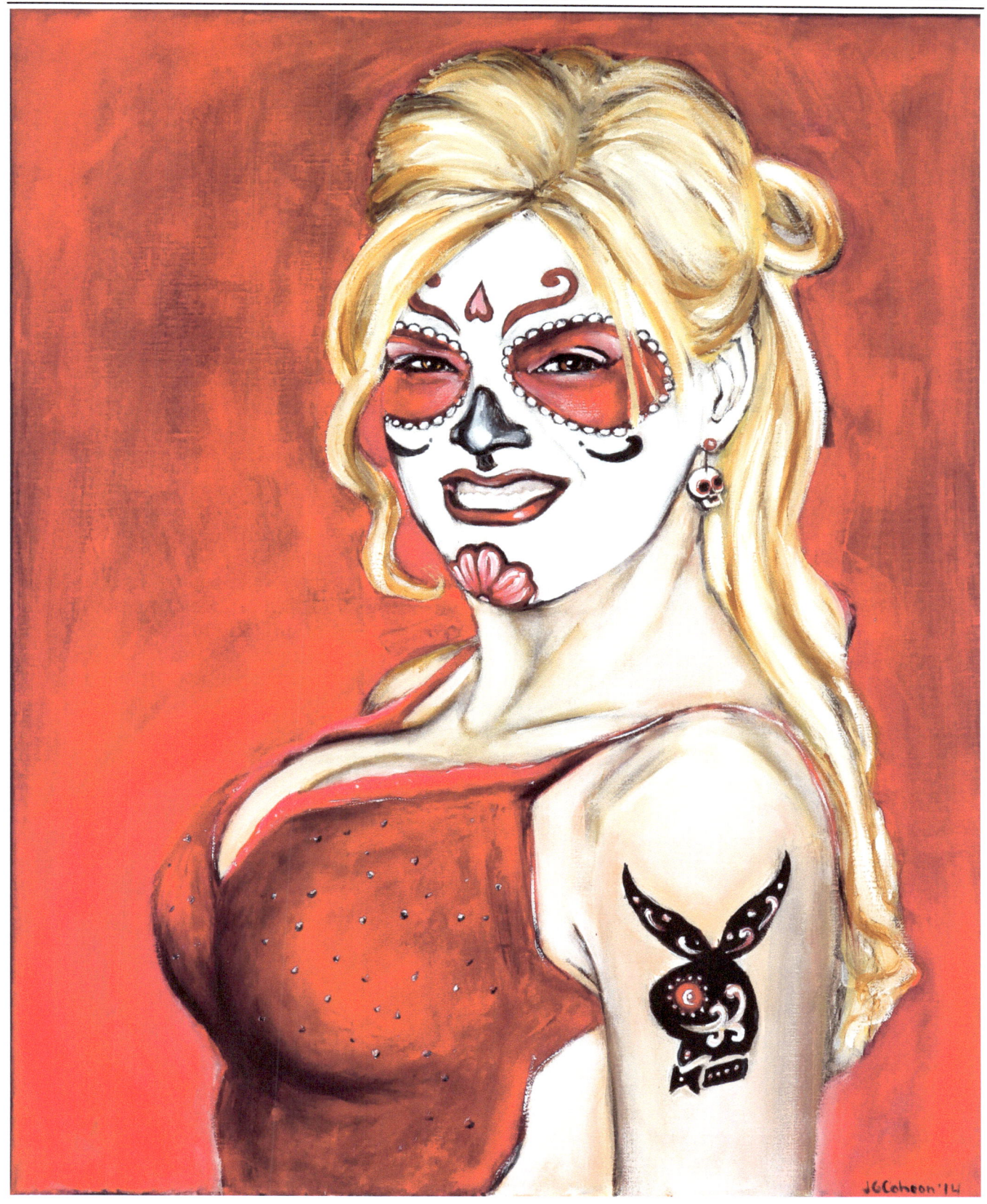

> # I want every little girl in the world to pick up a guitar and start screaming.
>
> ## Courtney Love

Courtney Love is an American musician, songwriter, actress and artist. She is the frontwoman of the rock band Hole, and the widow of grunge rocker Kurt Cobain, who committed suicide while they were married. While Love has been successful in her creative life, she has become a regular in the tabloids for her battles with substance abuse and her loud, outspoken nature. Her use of heroin resulted in the loss of custody of Love and Cobain's daughter, Frances Bean, with whom she has a difficult relationship. Love is a practicing Buddhist, and has worked to raise money for AIDS research and LGBT youth. She has spoken openly about being negatively compared with Yoko Ono, and being held responsible for Cobain's death by his fans.

Courtney Love, Dia de Los Muertos
Jennifer Gillooly Cahoon

Water Miscible oil paint on linen.
16" x 20"

From the artist: *Courtney Love is one of the bad girls of Rock 'N Roll. She has never been afraid to be true to herself, and say what is on her mind. She represents one of the early pieces in the new direction of my current series. Up until recently, I have only painted those who had passed. Here, the Day of the Dead symbolism is shown through segmented peep holes hovering over her eyes and hand of the very much alive Courtney Love. Within these niches, you get a glimpse into my interpretation of her inner essence.*

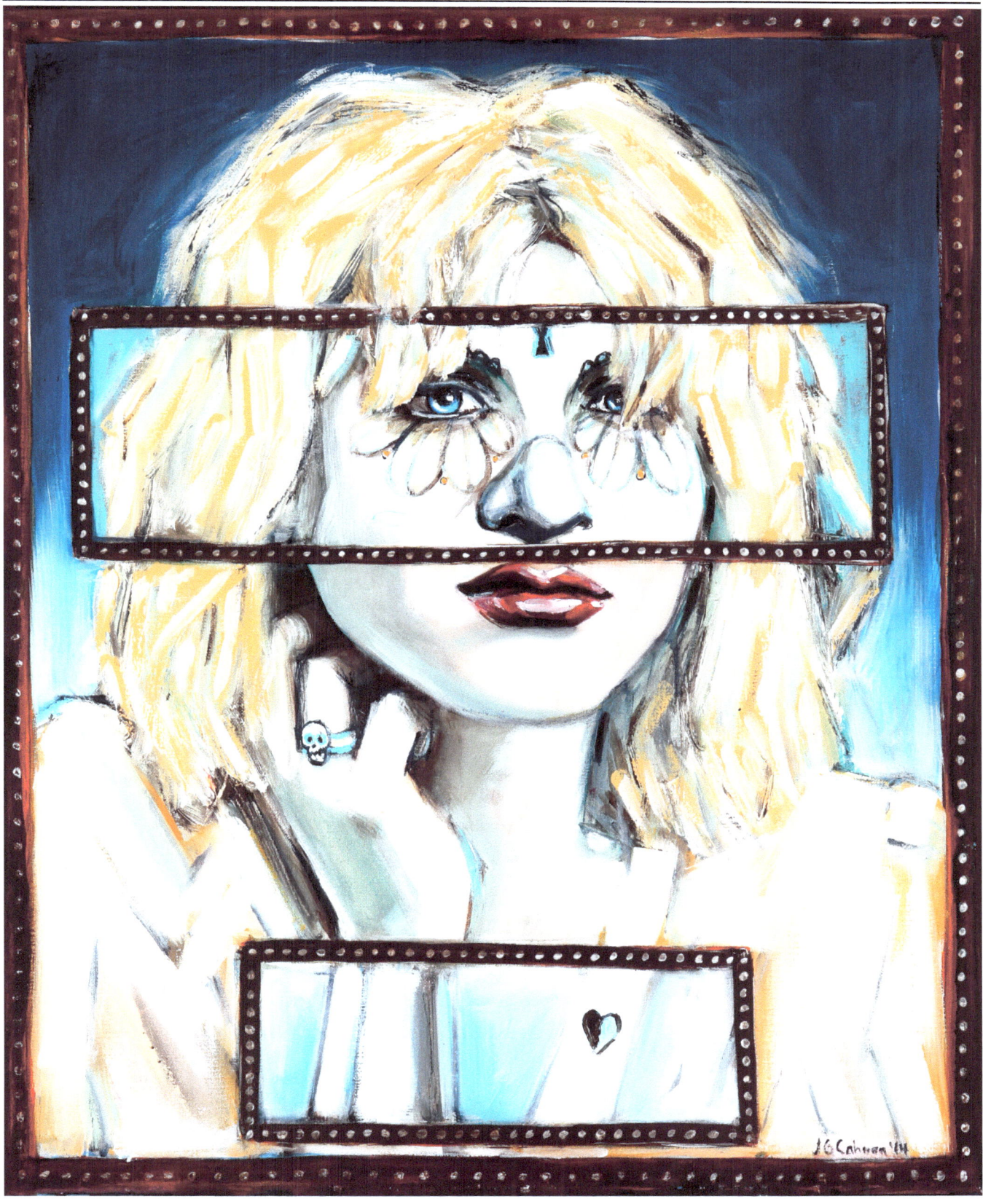

If you see somebody running down the street naked every single day, you stop looking up.

Stevie Nicks

Stevie Nicks is an American singer-songwriter who rose to fame as a member of the band Fleetwood Mac. She is known for her mystical image, billowing skirts, and long blonde hair, all of which have contributed to the rumor that she is a witch and involved in Wicca. During the 1980's, while pursuing her successful solo career, she entered the Betty Ford Clinic for chemical dependence, but remained addicted to tranquilizers through the early '90s. In the late '90s, Nicks detoxed, and reuinted with Fleetwood Mac for several albums and tours. Most recently, she has appeared in the cable drama American Horror Story: Coven.

Stevie Nicks with Sugar Skull
Jennifer Gillooly Cahoon

Acrylic paint on canvas.
22" x 28"

From the artist: *In this piece, a very young Stevie is depicted in one of her 1970s "witch" outfits and is holding a sugar skull, keeping it in line with the rest of the Dia de Los Muertos series.*

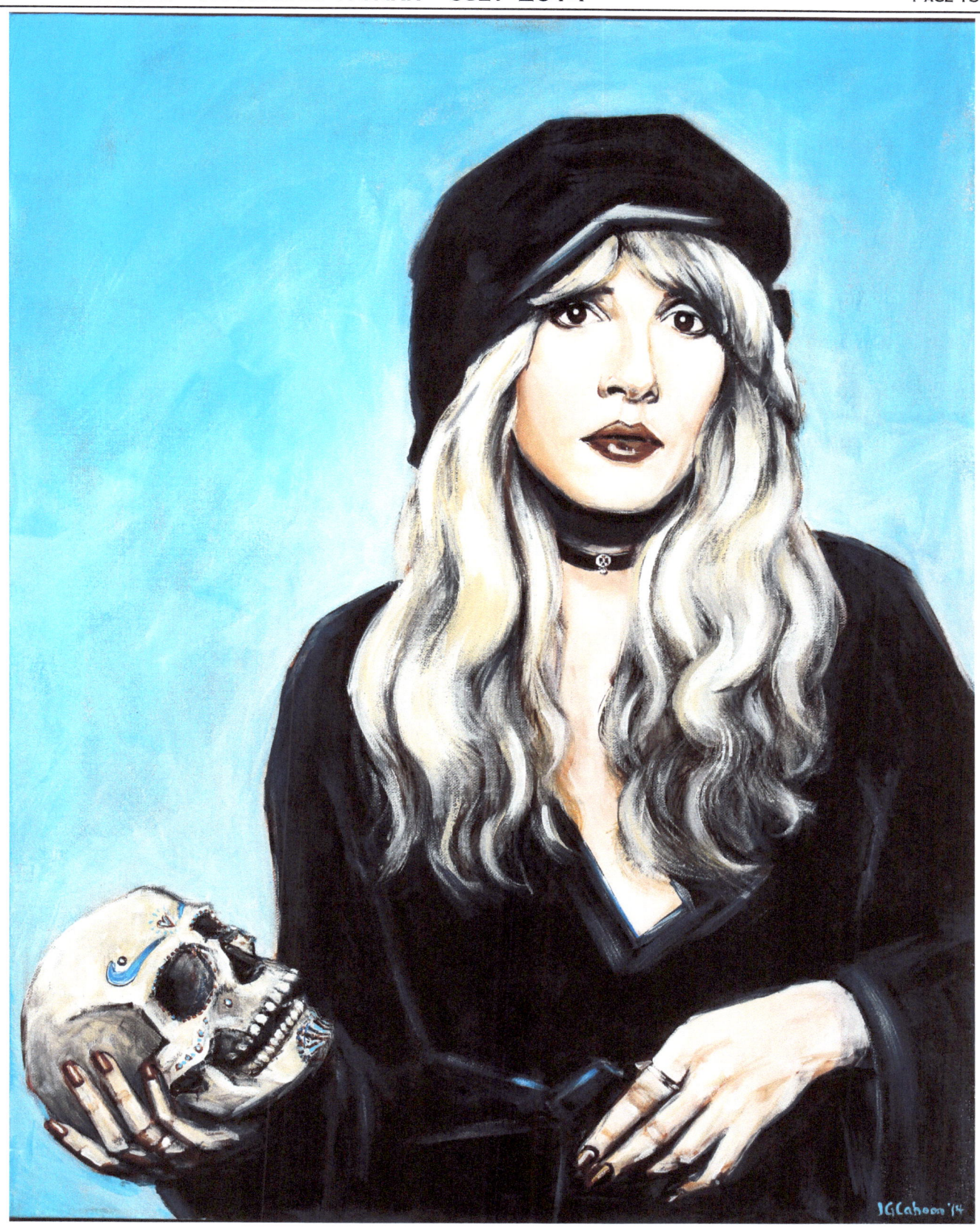

> # I have seen all.
> # I have heard all.
> # I have forgotten all.
>
> ## Marie Antoinette

Marie Antoinette was the Queen of France from 1774 to 1792, when she and her husband, Louis XVI, were deposed. Marie was tried and convicted of treason by the Revolutionary Tribunal, and executed by guillotine in 1793.

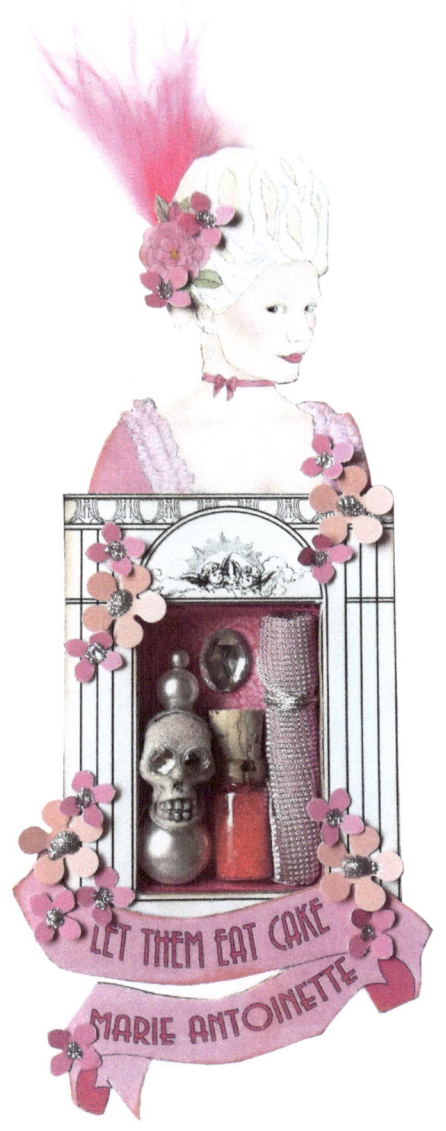

Marie Matchbox Shrine
Lisa Vollrath

Chipboard, paper, found objects.
2¾" X 7½"

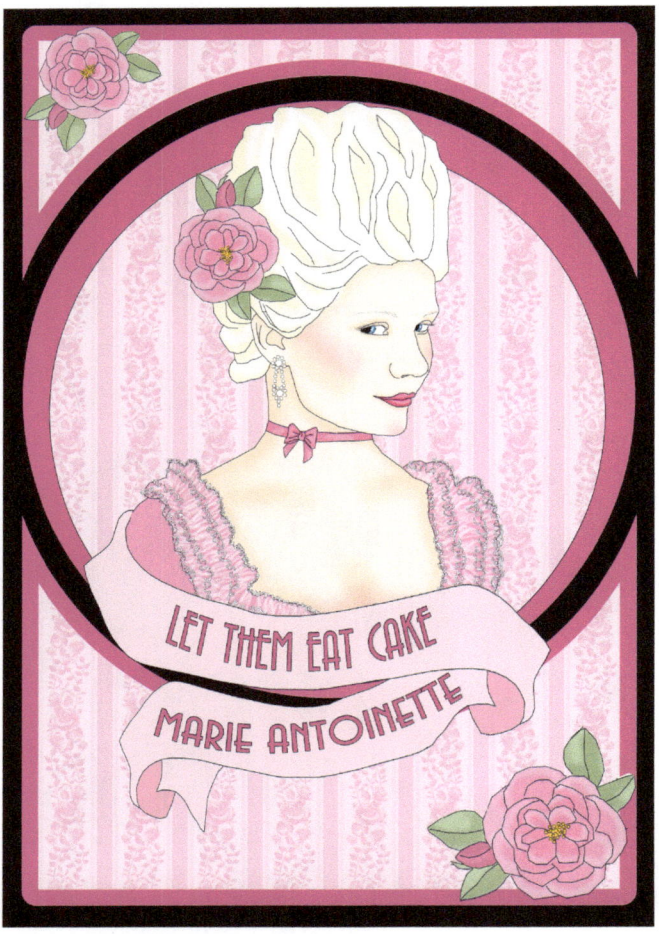

Sweet Marie
Lisa Vollrath

Digital illustration for
4" X 6" postcards.

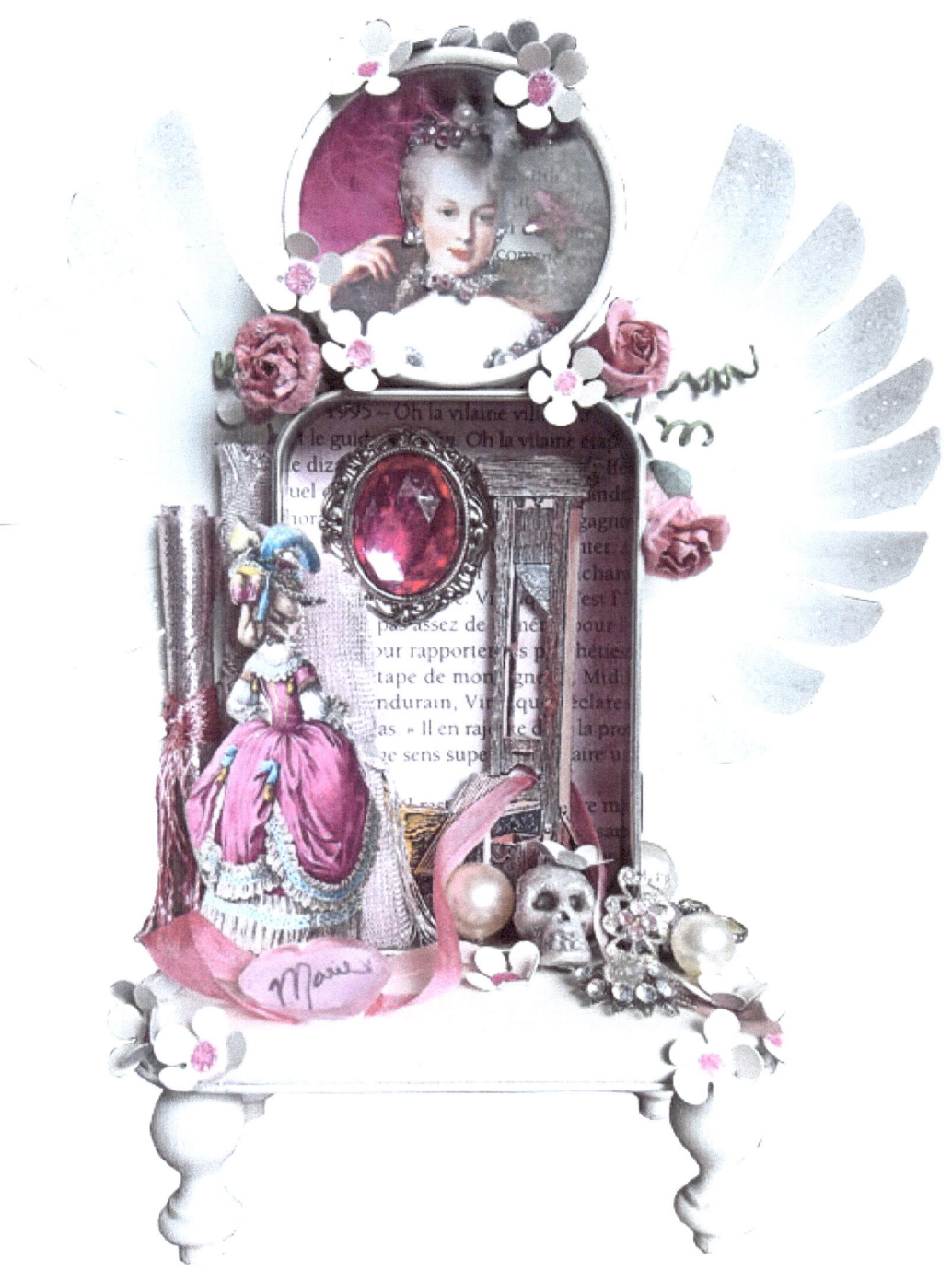

Winged Marie Shrine by Lisa Vollrath
Metal and found objects. 7¼" X 6¾" X 2¼"

From the artist: *I've always been fascinated by the opposing facets of Marie Antoinette's story: her frivolous, lacy excess and her horrible death. I combined those two themes in this shrine: pink and glittery, but with a skull and guillotine tucked amongst the finery.*

I am not afraid.

I was born to do this.

Joan of Arc

Joan of Arc was a French peasant girl who is considered a heroine of France, and a Roman Catholic saint. She was nicknamed The Maid of Orleans after being sent by King Charles VII on a relief mission to the siege of Orleans. After several battles, she was captured and handed over to the English, then put on trial for heresy, in part for wearing male clothing. She was found guilty, and burned at the stake in 1431, at the age of 19.

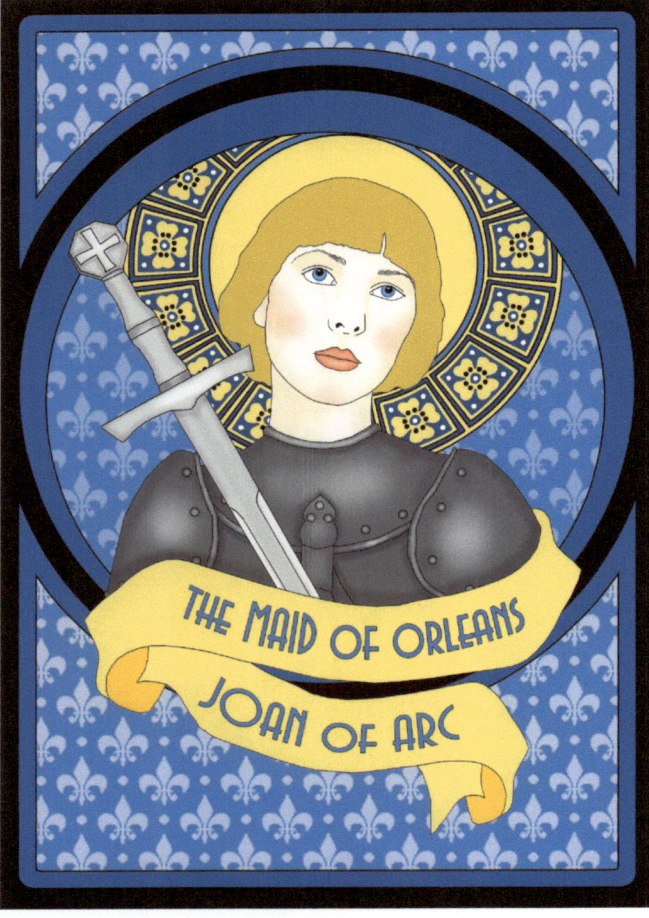

Joan of Arc
Lisa Vollrath

Digital illustration for
4" X 6" postcards.

Joan of Arc Shrine
Lisa Vollrath

Metal and found objects.
7¾" X 7½" X 2½"

From the artist: *I was happy to sacrifice a chain mail bracelet I wore in my 20s to include in this piece.*

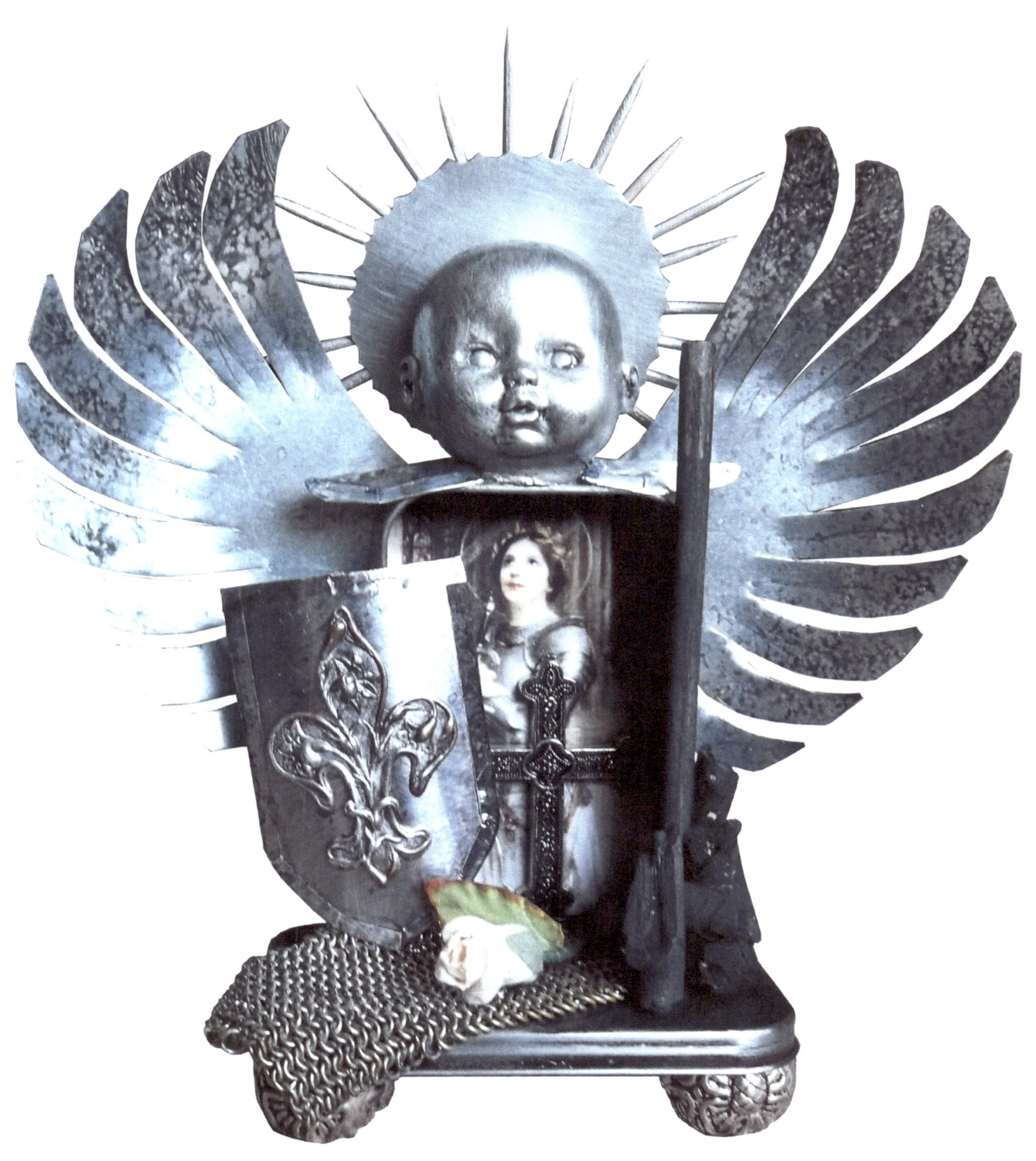

> ## If people knew the reasons for my fears, they would understand my pain.
>
> ### Lucrezia Borgia

Lucrezia Borgia was the daughter of Pope Alexander VI. Her family has become synonymous with ruthless politics, corruption and murder. Lucrezia was said to be adept at administering poison to her unwitting victims, using a hollow ring in which she secreted powders to pour into drinks. It was also supposed that she had incestuous relationships with both her father and her brother, Cesare. Despite these stories, very little is actually known about Lucrezia and her life, beyond the fact that she was married off to a succession of important and powerful men in order to advance her family's ambitions.

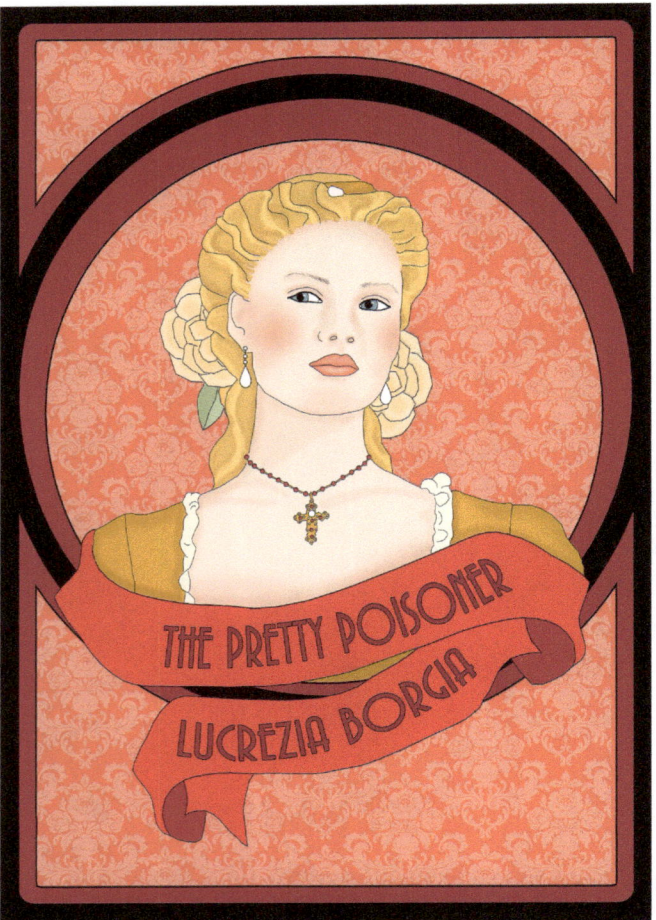

Lucrezia Borgia
Lisa Vollrath

Digital illustration for
4" X 6" postcards.

Lucrezia Borgia Shrine
Lisa Vollrath

Metal and found objects.
6¼" X 7" X 2¾"

From the artist: *I love having an excuse to include mysterious bottles, and a poisoner's ring into a piece. Lucrezia was such a fun subject for a shrine!*

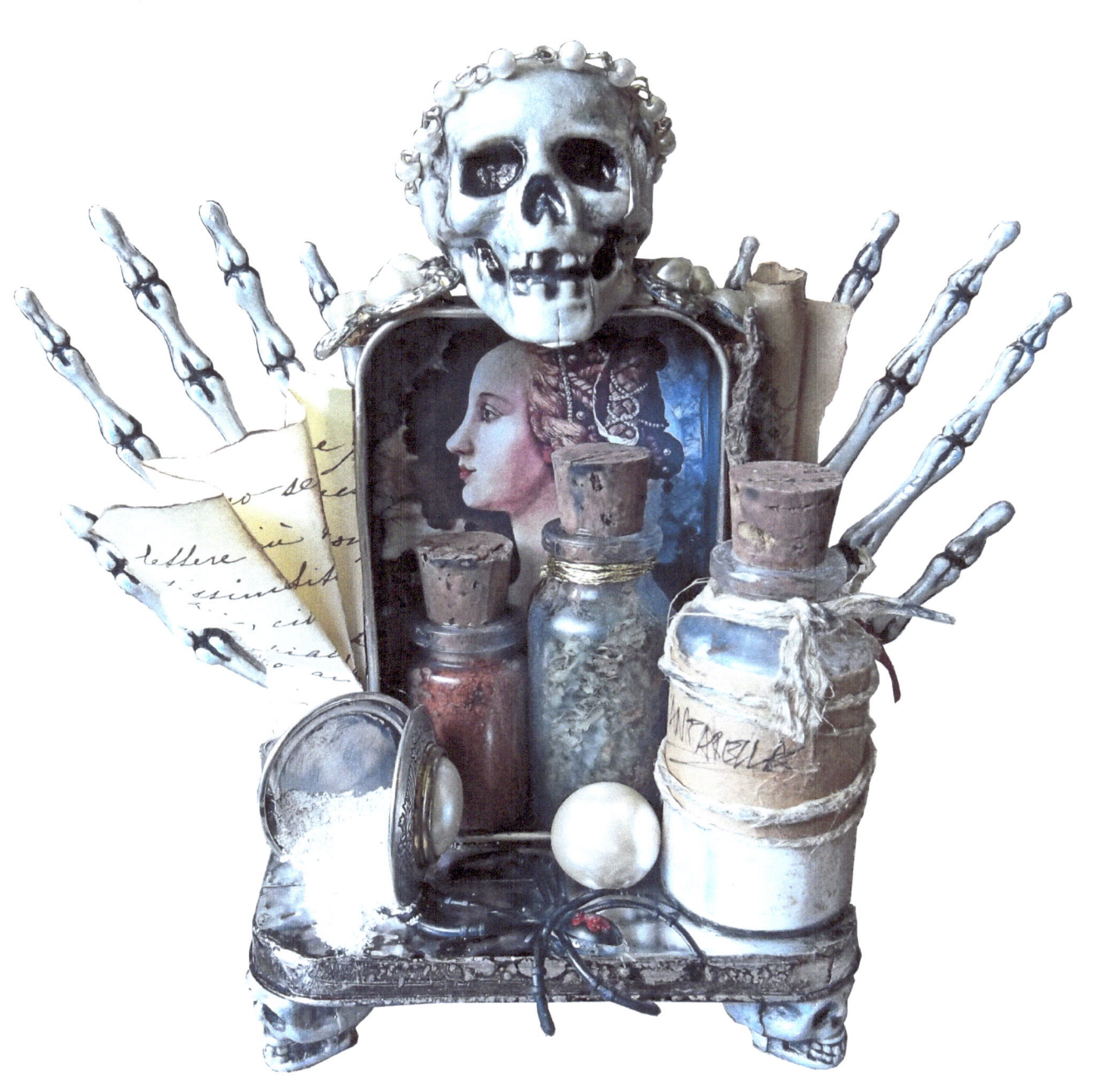

In thee, O lord, is my trust, let me never be confounded: if God be for us, who can be against us?

Mary I of England

Mary Tudor (Mary I of England) was the only surviving child of Henry VIII and his first wife, Catherine of Aragon. Mary was raised Catholic, while her father renounced the faith and founded the Church of England, in order to divorce her mother. When Henry's son, Edward, died in 1553 after just a few years on the throne, Mary became the first English queen to rule in her own right. Mary vowed to restore England to the Catholic faith, and during her reign, over 250 people were burned at the stake for religious dissent, earning her the name Bloody Mary. She died without an heir in 1558.

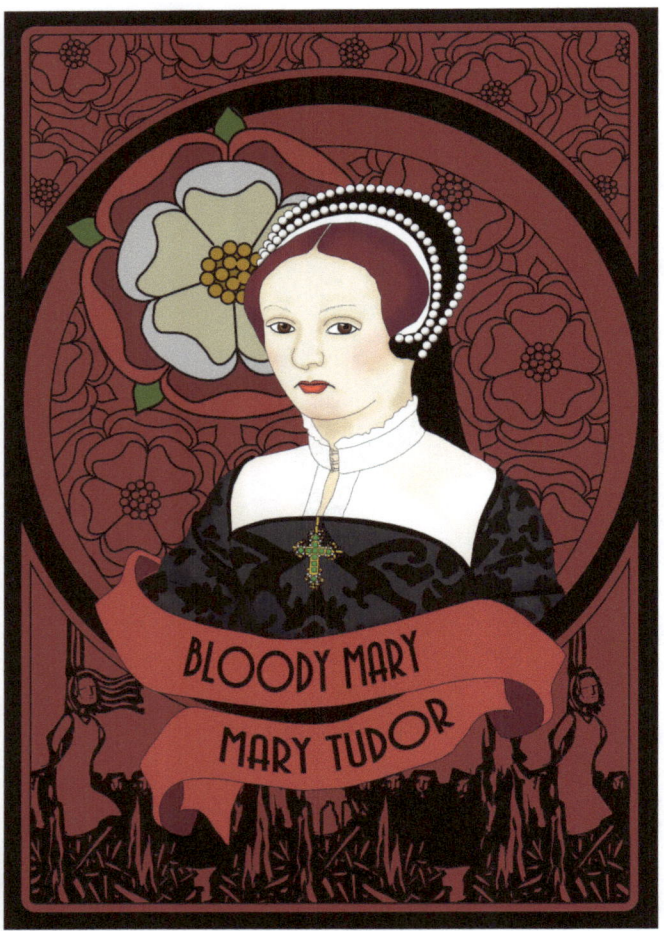

Mary Tudor
Lisa Vollrath

Digital illustration for
4" X 6" postcards.

Bloody Mary Matchbox Shrine
Lisa Vollrath

Chipboard, paper, found objects.
2¾" X 7"

From the artist: *I've always felt a little sorry for Mary. All she really wanted was to be a good Catholic, a good wife, and a good mother. She ended up burning people at the stake, driving her husband back to Spain, and dying without an heir.*

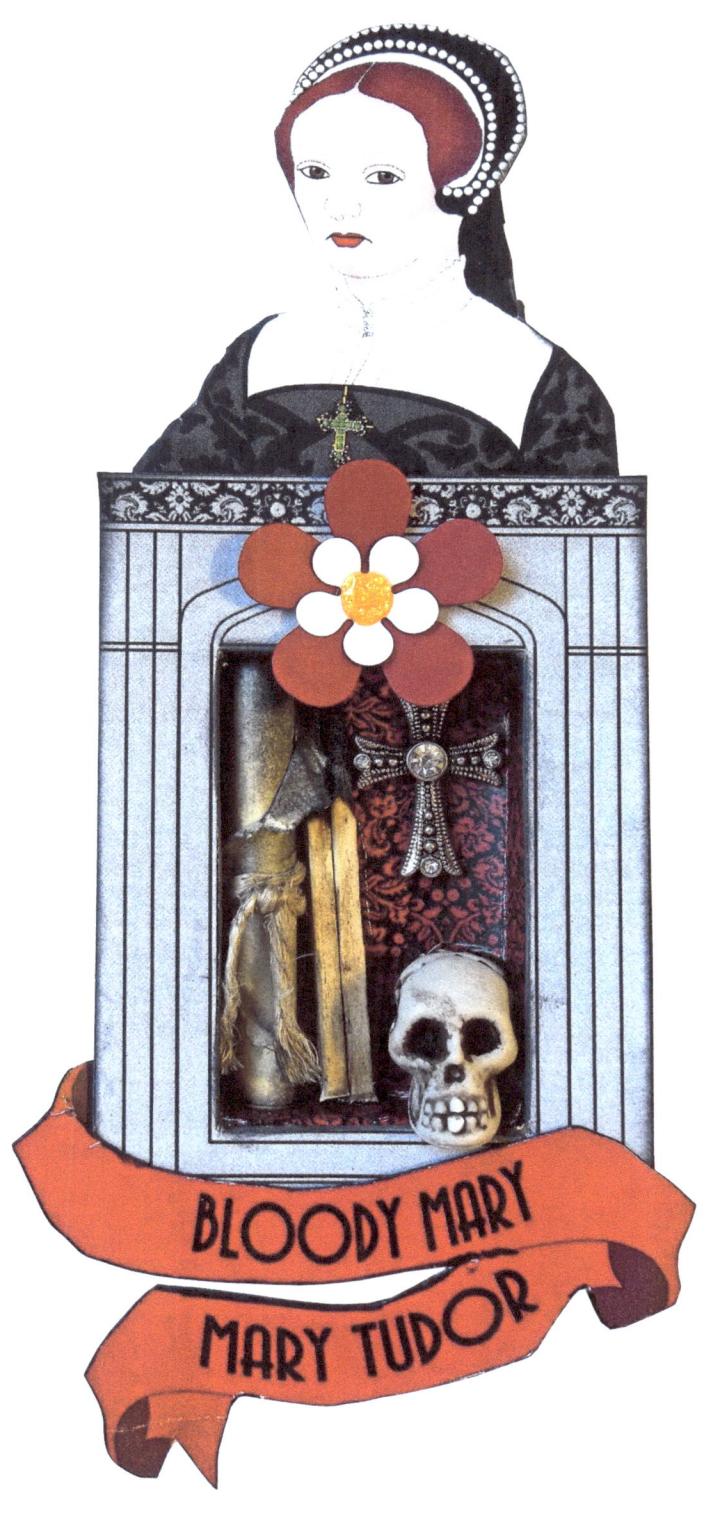

Lizzie Borden...is either the most injured of innocents or the blackest of monsters.

Julian Ralph, journalist, 1892

Lizzie Borden was 32 when she was tried and acquitted of the axe murders of her father and stepmother in 1892. While the case was widely covered in the press, Lizzie lived out her life in Fall River, Massachusetts, where the murders occurred, even though she was shunned by the residents of the town. After she was acquitted, no other suspects were charged and to this day, nobody knows who committed the murders. Lizzie died in Fall River in 1927.

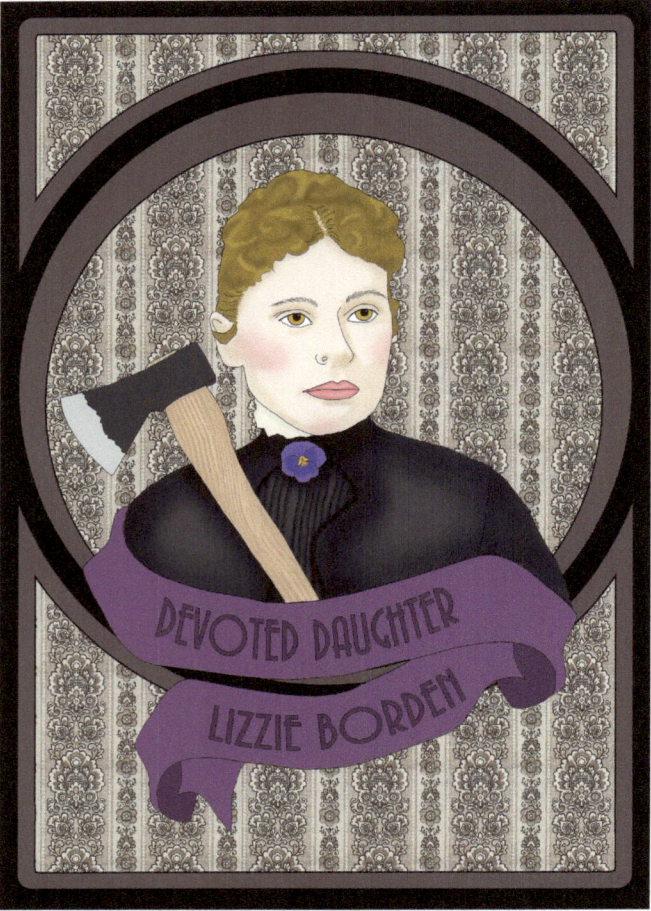

Lizzie Borden
Lisa Vollrath

Digital illustration for
4" X 6" postcards.

Lizzie Borden Matchbox Shrines
Lisa Vollrath

Chipboard, paper, found objects.

From the artist: *I love the story of Lizzie Borden. Did she do it? Who knows? It's one of those mysteries that will never be definitively solved.*

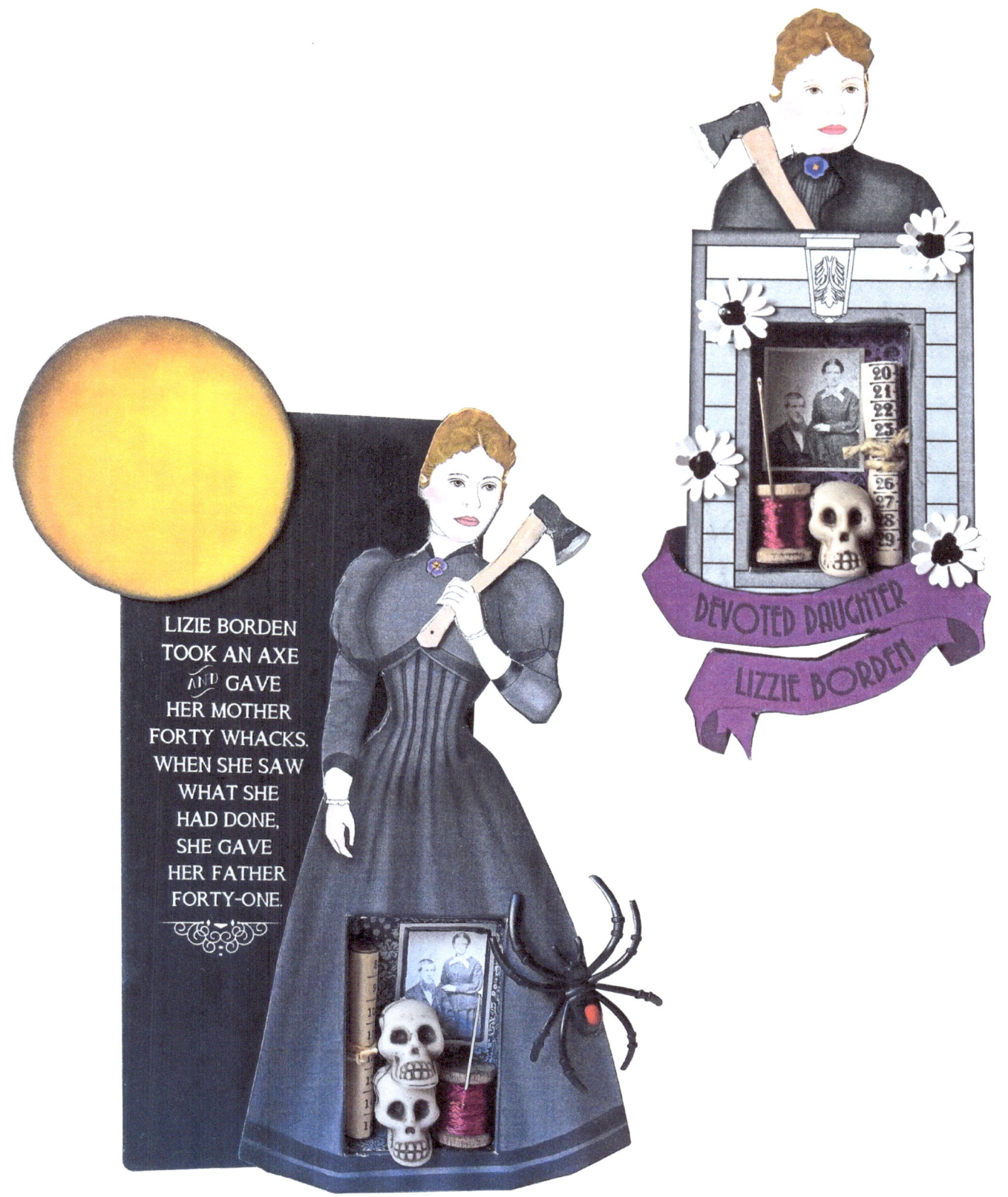

LIZIE BORDEN TOOK AN AXE AND GAVE HER MOTHER FORTY WHACKS. WHEN SHE SAW WHAT SHE HAD DONE, SHE GAVE HER FATHER FORTY-ONE.

DEVOTED DAUGHTER LIZZIE BORDEN

I am a woman who enjoys herself very much; sometimes I lose, sometimes I win.

Mata Hari

Mata Hari was a Dutch exotic dancer convicted by France of spying for the Germans during World War I. Because she was from the Netherlands, which was neutral, she could travel freely during the war, and her trips to and from France, through Spain and Great Britain, attracted attention. Accused and convicted of supplying information that caused the death of over 50,000 soldiers, she was executed by firing squad in 1917. German documents unsealed in the 1970s proved that Mata Hari was, in fact, a spy for Germany for the two years prior to her arrest.

Mata Hari Tins & Shrines
Lisa Vollrath

Metal tins, paper, found objects.
Assorted sizes.

From the artist: *Mata Hari was an exotic dancer who was a spy How could I not use her as a subject for a shrine?*

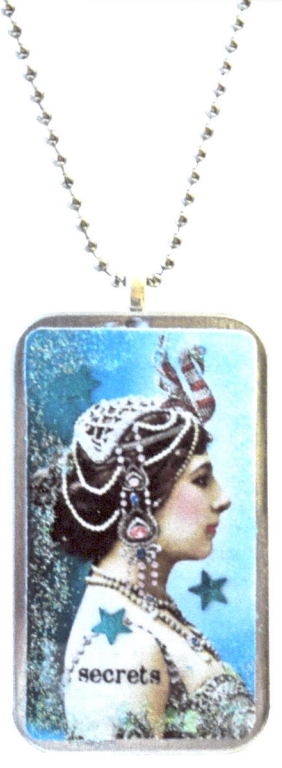

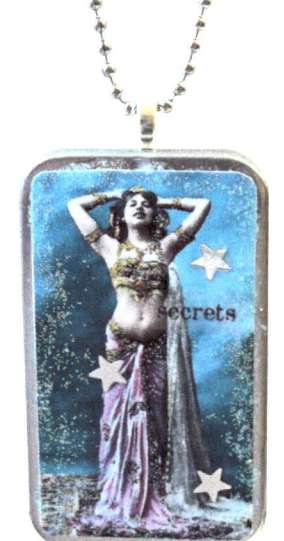

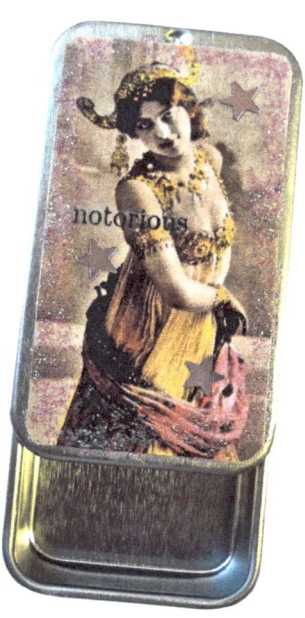

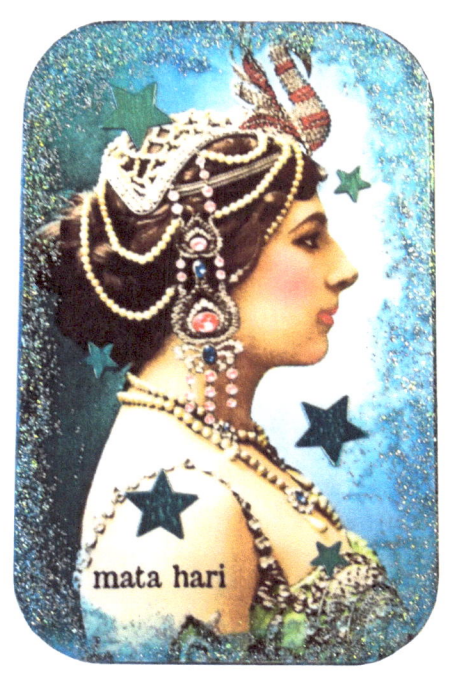

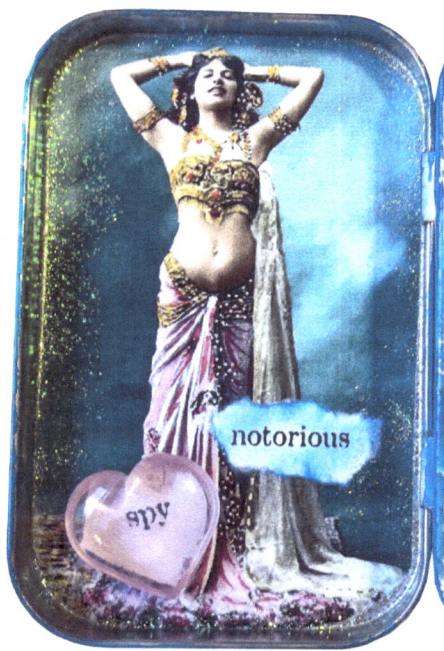

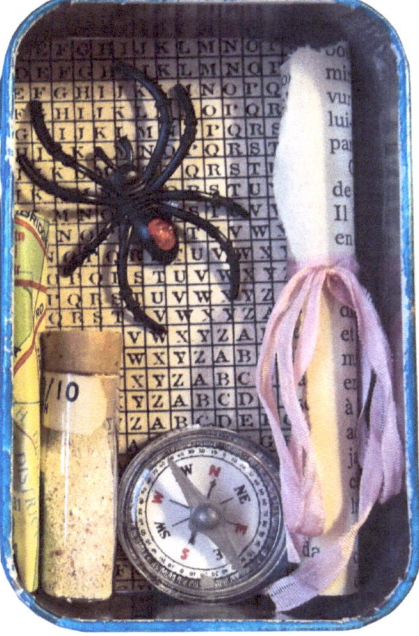

Cleopatra stood at one of the most dangerous intersections in history; that of women and power.

Stacy Schiff, *Cleopatra: A Life*

Cleopatra (Cleopatra VII Philopator), the final active pharoh of Ancient Egypt, ruled from 69BC to 30BC. She was a member of the Ptolemaic dynasty, of Greek ancestry, and spoke both Greek and Egyptian. She had a son with Julius Caesar to solidify her hold on the Egyptian throne, and after Caesar's death, joined forces with Mark Antony against Julius Caesar Octavianus. She bore three children with Antony before losing the Battle of Actium to Octavian's forces. Antony committed suicide after the defeat, and Cleopatra followed him, killing herself with a traditional asp bite.

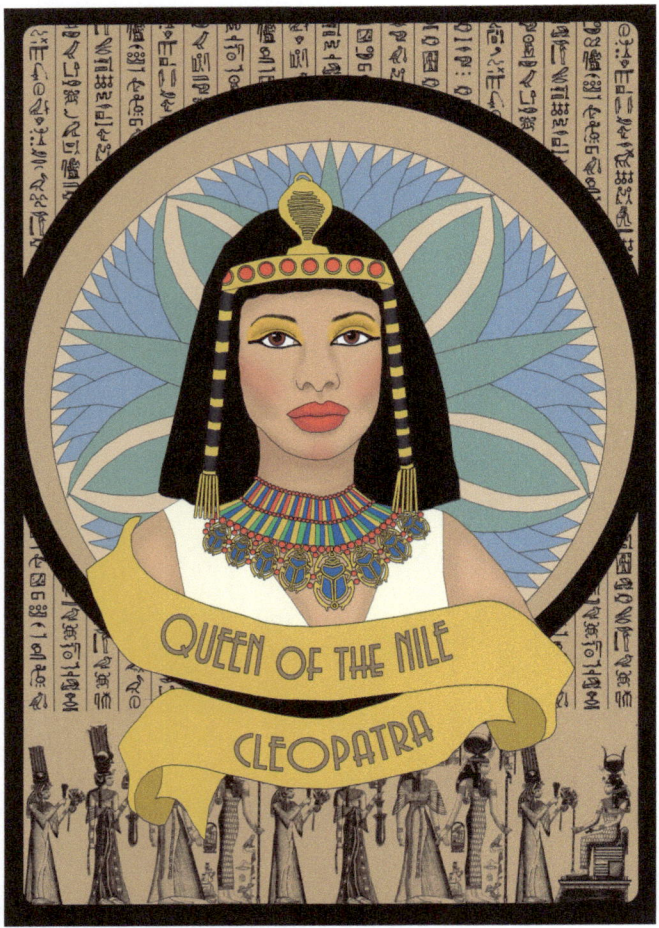

Cleopatra
Lisa Vollrath

Digital illustration for
4" X 6" postcards.

Kiss My Asp Statement Necklace
Barbe Saint John

Necklace is 20" long.
Pendant is 3 ½" wide.

From the artist: *This is a big, bold and beautiful statement necklace honoring a woman who ruled a turbulent country and looked fabulous while doing it.*

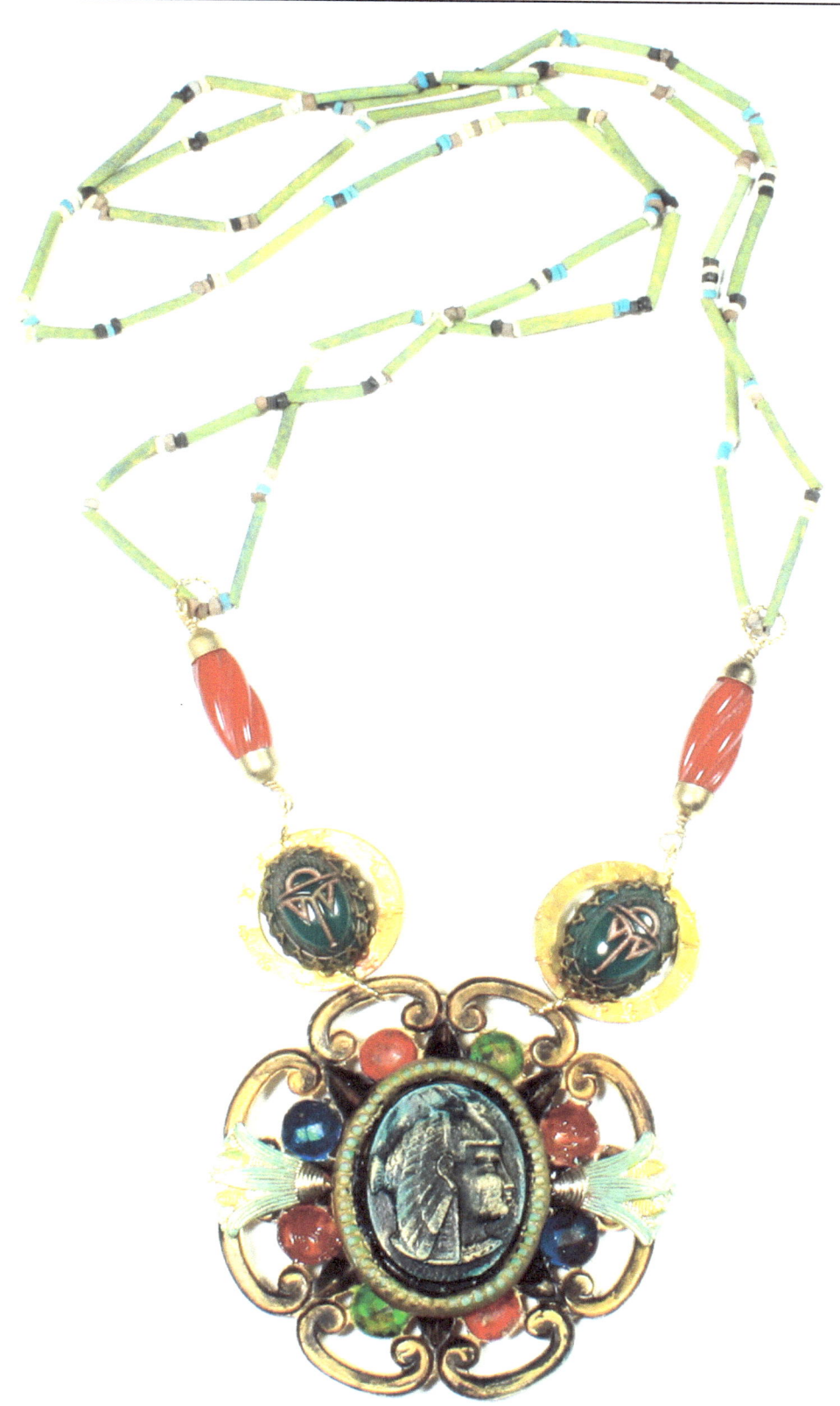

You find out who your real friends are when you're involved in a scandal.

Elizabeth Taylor

Elizabeth Taylor was a British-American actress. She began acting as a child, and became one of the great screen stars of Hollywood's Golden age. She was known for her beauty and distinctive violet eyes---and for the fact that she married eight times to seven husbands, and had many romances with famous men. Taylor had a role in sparking the sexual revolution of the 1960s, and was one of the first major Hollywood stars to pose motly nude in Playboy. She was also among the first actresses to remove her clothes onscreen. In her later years, Dame Elizabeth was a tireless advocate for HIV/AIDS projects and charities, and was the cofounder of amfAR.

LIZ
Jean Mirre

Digital collage.
80cm x 60cm

From the artist: *I like portraits, like the ones I see in magazines or on the Internet. I want them to be new, so I change them until they become unfamiliar, as if never seen before.*

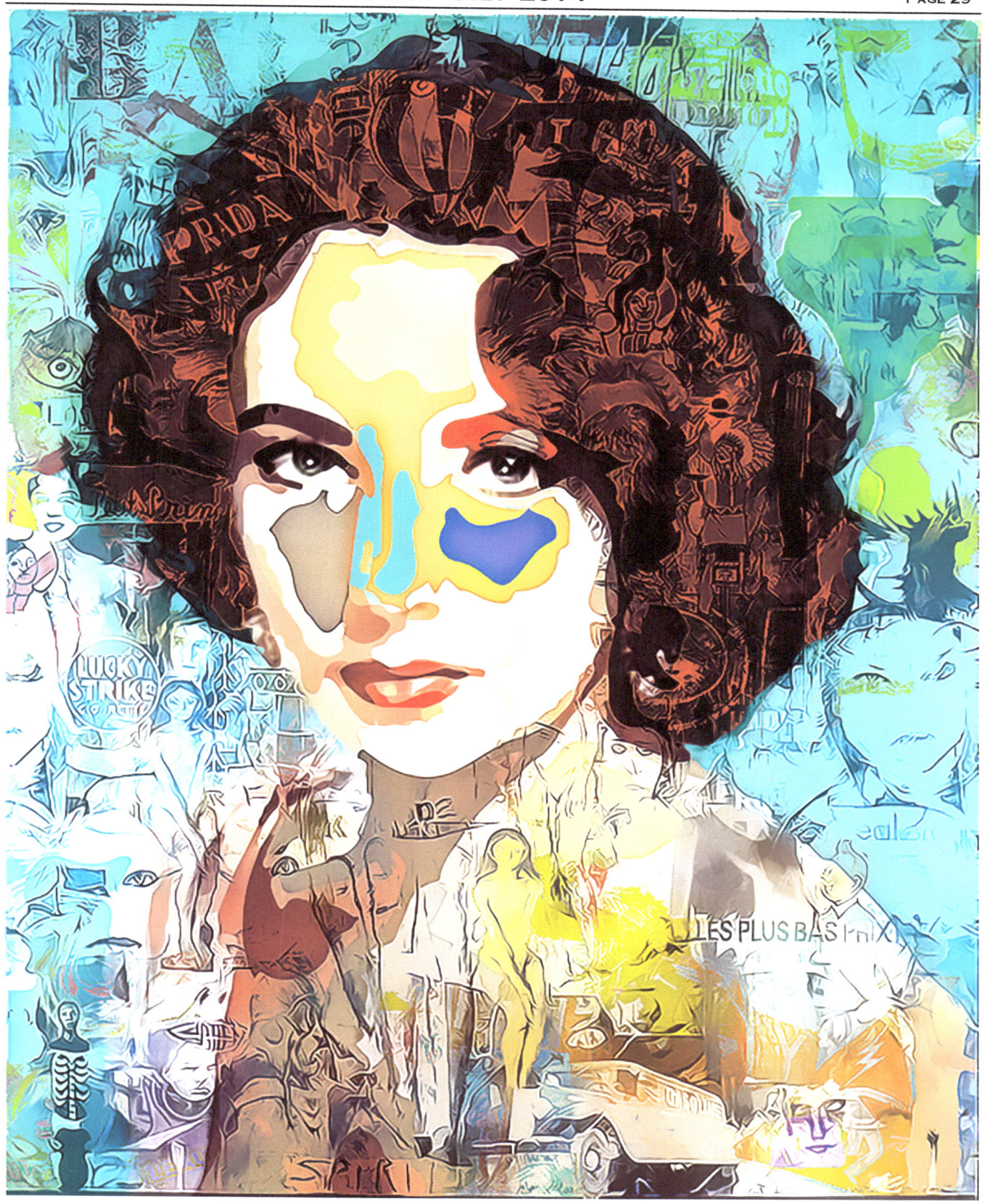

> **Love is a fire.**
> **But whether it is going to**
> **warm your hearth**
> **or burn down your house,**
> **you can never tell.**
>
> **Joan Crawford**

Joan Crawford was an American film and television star, most noted for her portrayal of rags-to-riches characters in the 1920s and '30s, and for her Academy Award winning role in the 1945 film *Mildred Pierce*. Frustrated with the parts she was given early in her career, she set out to promote herself, first has the ultimate flapper in silent films, and then as a box office star, eventually becoming the highest paid actress in Hollywood. Crawford was married four times, and adopted four children. Her daughter Christina wrote *Mommy Dearest* in 1978, chronicling the abuse the children suffered in Crawford's care.

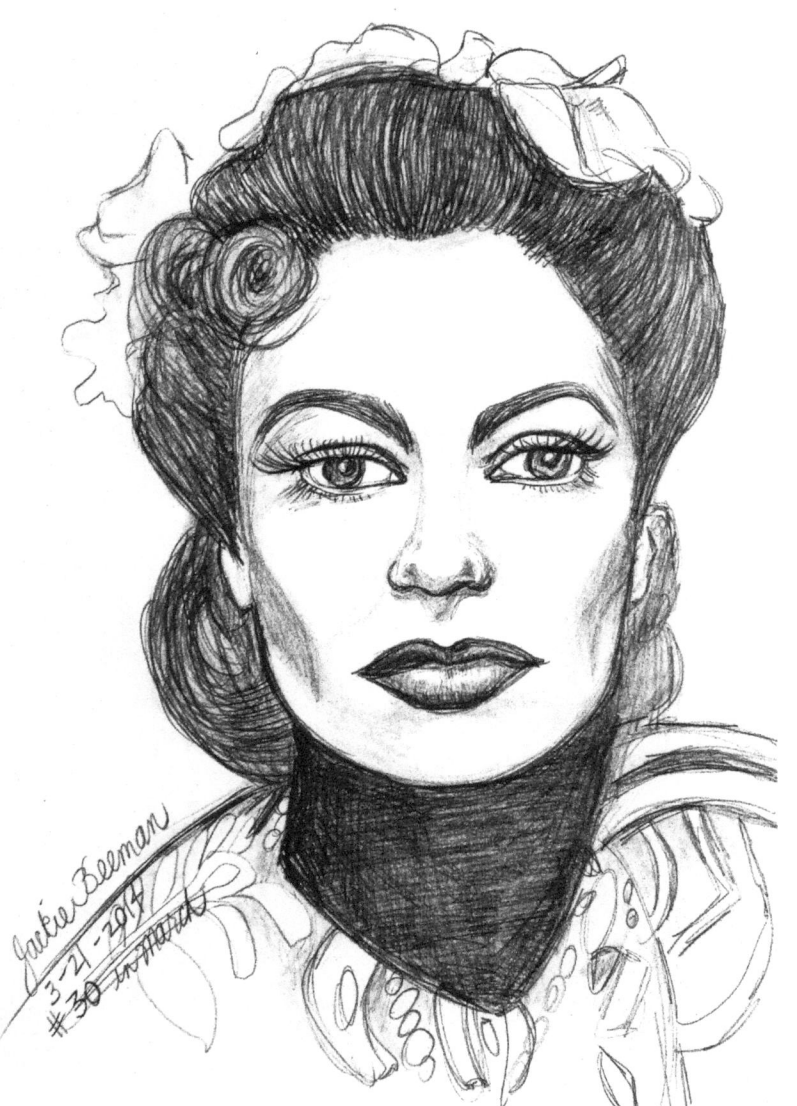

Secrets Hide in the Dark
Jackie Beeman

Graphite on paper.
5.5" x 8.5"

From the artist: *Joan Crawford was voted the tenth greatest female star in the history of American cinema by the American film institute. Her reputation was tarnished when her daughter alleged a lifetime of physical and emotional abuse at the hand of her mother.*

www.ingramcontent.com/pod-product-compliance
Lightning Source LLC
Chambersburg PA
CBHW050415180526
45159CB00005B/2290